Factious Disorders: Fantasies and Facts

(Munchausen Syndrome

and

Munchausen by Proxy)

Table of Contents

Abstract

Factitious Disorders (better knowns as Munchausen Syndrome and Munchausen Syndrome by Proxy) involve a person intentionally injuring themselves or their children mostly for the sake of getting attention for themselves. Some of these injuries are disfiguring. Some of these injuries are life-threatening. Some of these injuries are fatal. This book will discuss the incidents and dynamics of these activities and the legal ramifications for the person, mental health practitioners and the legal system. Be advised that some of the intentional harm is quite graphic but I have intentionally withheld the most gruesome photos available in the sake of civility.

Introduction

The Diagnostic and Statistical Manual-5 (DSM-5) (2013) includes two disorders titled "Factitious Disorder Imposed on Self" and "Factitious Disorder Imposed on Another". In all previous DSMs starting with the DSMIII, the disorders were labeled "Chronic Factitious Disorder with Physical Symptoms" and "Chronic Factitious Disorders with Psychological Symptoms".

The DSM-5 Desk Reference states the criteria for Factitious Disorder Imposed on Self are a) falsification of physical or psychological signs or symptoms, induction of injury or disease, associated with identified deception, b) the individual presents himself or herself to others as ill, impaired or injured, c) the deceptive behavior is evident even in the absence of obvious external rewards, and d) the behavior is not better explained by another mental disorder such as delusional disorder or another psychotic disorder (page 165).

The DSM5 states the criteria for Factitious Disorder Imposed On Another are a) falsification of physical or psychological signs or symptoms, or induction of injury or disease, in another, associated with identified deception, b) the individual presents another individual (victim) to others as ill, impaired or injured, c) the deceptive behavior is evident even in the absence of obvious external rewards, and d) the behavior is not better explained by another mental disorder such as delusional disorder or another psychotic disorder (page 165).

Whereas the previous DSMs mentioned hospitalization or seeking hospitalization as a necessary criterion for either diagnosis, the DSM-5 does not require any aspect of hospitalization, merely specifying "single episode" or "recurrent episodes".

This pattern of self-harm wherein individuals fabricate histories, signs, and symptoms of illness was originally identified by Dr. Richard Asher (1951). He wrote "Here is described a common syndrome which most doctors have seen, but about which little has been written. Like the famous Baron von Munchausen, the persons affected have always travelled widely; and their stories, like those attributed to him, are both dramatic and untruthful. Accordingly, the syndrome is respectfully dedicated to the Baron, and named after him." The behaviors have continued to be labeled Munchausen's Syndrome (MS) or Munchausen's by Proxy (MbP) in the general public literature but these names barely occur in the DSMs. It has also been called "hospital addiction syndrome", "thick chart syndrome", fabricated-induced illness (fii) or "hospital hopper syndrome". Gross (2008) also mentioned alternative names of "pathomimia," "peregrinating problem patients," "ipsepathogenic patients," "nosocomotropism," and "Van Gogh Syndrome". Schoenfeld et al., (1987) reported they and their diseases have also been labeled "pseudopatients", "laparatomophilia migrans", "hemoptysis merchants", "hemmorhagia hysteroinica", "neurologica diabolica", "dermatitis autogenica", "hyperpyrexia pigmentatica", "peripathic pseudoporphyria", "metabolic malingerers", and "polysurgery syndrome".

In 1977, English pediatrician Roy Meadow published a report of a new type of child abuse, in which mothers consciously invented stories of illness in their children that they frequently but sometimes erroneously substantiated as having been created by the mother by inducing physical symptoms in the child (Meadow, 1977). Carrying the parallel with Munchhausen even further, Meadow labeled this destructive dynamic "Munchausen Syndrome by Proxy" (MbP). He asserted that mothers suffering from MbP were willfully hurting and sometimes even killing their children, claiming that "one sudden infant death is a tragedy, two is suspicious, and three is murder, until proved otherwise" (Meadow, 1977). This position became known as "Meadow's Law" and for a time, became the rule of thumb for British child protection agencies. Munchausen by Proxy has also been called "Polle syndrome", so named after Munchausen's only son.

These disorders are not solely present in America or Great Britain. Articles have been published about their occurrence in China (Yuan, et al., 2012), Israel (Leiba, et al., 2012), France (Beis, et al., 2012), Turkey (Tüfekçi, et al., 2011; Tamay, et al, 2007), Sweden (Okuniewska, et al., 2011), Greece (Zibis, et al., 2010), Saudi Arabia (Al-Owain, et al., 2009), Taiwan (Lee, et al, 2010), Japan (Kume & Sakata, 2010; Fujiwara et al., 2008; Tochigi, et al.,2007), Canada (Archambault-Grenier, et al., (2010), Germany (Klepper et al., 2007; Feldman et al., 2007), Australia (Kaplan, 2008), Spain (Conception & Garcia-Alba, 2008), Austria (Tran, 2006), Netherlands (Dute, 2003), New Zealand (Denny et al., 2001) and Sultanate of Oman (Bappal et al., 2001). The reader will note that there were no identified articles published about cases from Africa, Antarctica, or South America. No other authors have commented on that absence, no research has been done on it and speculation as to why these locations do not report any cases of either disorder are purely speculative at this point.

While some authors postulated three body systems as targets for MS or MbP, the body organ or systems that are victimized in both MS and MBP disorders encompass all possible bodily systems and organs. These include nose and cheeks (Yuan et al., 2012), kidneys (Leiba, et al., 2012), eyes (Lin et al., 2012), abdominal muscles (Beis et al, 2012), nipples (Tüfekçi, et al., 2011), subdura (too many to cite), blood sugar levels (Kucuker et al., 2010), forearm (Zibis et al, 2010), central nervous system (Lee et al., 2009), gastrointestinal tract (Kume and Sakata, 2010; Tamay et al., 2007), bone marrow (Caocci et al., 2008), lungs (Korturk et al., 2006), immune system (Warner, 2005), blood vessels (Tasic et al, 2005), heart (Park et al., 2004), pathological desire for amputation of a limb (Bensler & Paauw, 2003), sleep (Hood and Harbord, 2002), multi-organ cystic fibrosis (Highland & Flume, 2002), female reproductive system (Azado & Essen, 2002), immune system (Berberoğlu, 2000), generalized childhood development (Elder and Kaplan, 2000), neck and jaw (Altman and Gardner, 1998), anorexia nervosa (Honjo, 1996), bulimia (Bulik et al., 1996), and larynx (Patterson et al., 1974).

The cautious reader of the extensive list above may wonder how bone marrow can be the subject of self-harm. This system was targeted by a woman who submitted falsified medical records from several real medical facilities purporting she had need for bone-marrow transplants when she in fact did not need any. Bone marrow grafts or transplants can be extremely painful and the risk of osteomyelitis (infection of the bone and bone marrow) is present with risk for amputation of the limb if infection in the bone or bone marrow occurs.

The neurological problems include induced or claimed seizures. On a morbid, life-threatening, life-changing level, Barker (1962) reported two cases where unnecessary frontal lobotomies were sought by MS patients and performed.

In addition to all of the variations mentioned above about different countries, continents and body targets, the methods of inducing real physical damage to the body is widely varied beyond the crude and most common methods of hitting with hammers, falls, jumps, placing caustics on the skin and doing subcutaneous injections of feces, urine and saliva under the skin. Other less common methods include the following from the references already cited (without their citation for the sake of brevity): injecting egg white, injecting herbs, feeding insecticides, intentional frostbite, inserting flashlights and spray cans into the rectum, faking medical records, lying about medical records, injecting fermented beans, laundry detergent poisoning, excessive use of antidiuretics, abusing anesthetics, insulin, Sulfonylurea compounds; overdosing ipecac, overdosing amitriptyline, planting worms in feces, putting drain-clog-removal chemicals in body orifices, eating lead and eating rat poison. The range of lethality of these agents and activities spans from the mere "attention-getting" to excruciatingly painful, gruesomely fatal and disfiguring.

Before dealing more with either syndrome, one must differentiate true MS and MbP from two other similar problems: malingering and Ganser Syndrome. Malingering is considered the intentional production of false or grossly exaggerated physical or psychological symptoms, motivated by external incentives such as avoiding military duty, avoiding work, obtaining financial compensation, evading criminal prosecution or obtaining drugs. Both MS and MbP have an absence of any "obvious" *external* (this writer's italics) reward as those mentioned above for malingering.

In regards to Ganser Syndrome, Schneider (2013) reported, "The most well-recognized symptom of Ganser syndrome is the so-called symptom of approximate answers (alternately designated in the literature by the German terms vorbeireden [talking past], vorbeigehen [to pass by], or danebenreden [talking next to]). Here, the patient responds to questions with an incorrect answer, but by the nature of the answer reveals an understanding of the question posed. This can be illustrated by the patient answering "3" when asked, "How many legs has a horse?" or "black" when asked "What color is snow?" or "Tuesday" when asked "What is the day after Sunday?" Frequently, the patient answers a number of questions with these odd approximate answers. This is in direct contrast to answers that are simply nonsensical, perseverative, or otherwise inappropriate." Schneider (2013) suggested there is often a malingering aspect to people who exhibit these types of behaviors.

Although approximate answers may be the most obvious of the symptoms, Ganser was clear that the syndrome included other important components. In all 3 of his patients he observed a time-limited condition that involved a clouding of consciousness that resolved rather suddenly, leaving only a residual amnesia for the events occurring while symptomatic. He referred to this as a "hysterical twilight state." He also described hallucinations in all 3 patients (which he assumed to be present from their behavior, not from patient complaints), as well as so-called hysterical stigmata. By this last statement, Ganser is referring to symptoms we would today associate with a conversion disorder. Ganser found sensory changes involving decreased reactivity to pinprick in all three patients, and in one patient he found the areas that were hyperalgesic to change depending on the day. He further described another case in the literature where the patient displayed "intractable paralysis and sensory disturbances." Although Ganser Syndrome has some components of physical dysfunction it clearly does not involve true, severe physical self-inflicted injuries found in the MS/MbP process.

This author has encountered some people in the general public with classic Munchausen tendencies of making very improbable claims. However, these story-tellers violated the "absence of obvious reward" factor so they would more likely be considered as malingering. The first person telling these far-fetched stories was a Caucasian male in his mid-50s. He claimed he was a Green Beret and fought in Viet Nam. He also claimed he and his Special Forces unit could infiltrate enemy positions and cut the throats of every-other enemy without making a sound or letting their victims cry out. This is impossible since death by slashed throat is never instantaneous or completely quiet. He also claimed he had been given a special mandate from a national American leader to design a new mental health paradigm for America, had received the Medal of Honor from the CIA (false-only the President awards that) and that the Medal of Honor was placed on the wall of honor at CIA headquarters in Langley, Virginia, so only he or fellow CIA operatives could ever view it. His external motivation seemed to be obtaining money, admiration and acceptance.

The second was a low-functioning, sporadically employed Caucasian male in his early 40s. He claimed his family owned a castle in Scotland but he could not afford money for a pack of cigarettes in America. He also claimed he had put out a grease fire at a restaurant with his bare hands without getting burned, had handled an entire Mother's Day restaurant crowd by himself without any other help (because all of the other workers had not shown up), could light a match being held in somebody's mouth with a pistol at 50 yards and reported to his girlfriend on a daily basis that he had almost got killed at work that day. This man was busy manipulating his girlfriend, his children and other people to get anything he could get from them.

The third person was a Caucasian, adult male in his early 40s whose DD214 (the standard military service record) listed his status as "machinist mate" without service overseas but who claimed he had been was a star athlete in high school. He also claimed he was on his high school's state-champion in swimming, had been a star athlete at a military academy before going into the military, a Special Forces *and* Navy seal operative during the American military actions titled Desert Storm and Operation Iraqi Freedom. He claimed he was a cross-trained as a medical corpsman, had people die in his arms, and had a father who was an internationally famous art appraiser who had an advanced degree in Art from a prestigious university in England. He claimed he had drown briefly during Navy Seal training, was on search and rescue teams, had seen people shoot themselves, set themselves on fire, jump to their death, and he had broken both feet, dislocated both shoulders, broken his nose and had barb-wire cuts received during combat. He claimed that he became a licensed stock broker after he got out of the military but was currently unemployed and had not been employed for several years. He also claimed his first wife got cancer and died and his current girlfriend just got raped by four illegal immigrants. He only related all of this information to me because he was filing for service-connected disability due to mental problems (claimed auditory and visual hallucinations). However, his hallucinations were not clinically typical, he showed no distress about the hallucinations, he showed no distress about anything he was talking about and he showed no physical or mental characteristics of a battle-hardened combat veteran. Previous evaluators had repeatedly commented on the "unlikely" nature of claims has he told them but never diagnosed him with Factitious Disorder. His goal also seemed to be to undeservedly obtain money and prestige from people around him.

However, some people really do hurt themselves or their children for secondary gain. This article will review Baron Von Munchhausen, the man, his myths, the psychological phenomenon of the Munchausen disorders, treatment, case management and forensic issues. It does not claim to be exhaustive, relying on data retrieved by an EBSCOhost search of the terms "Munchausen syndrome" in June of 2014.

The Man

Hieronymus Carl Friedrich Baron von Munchhausen was born May 11, 1720, and died February 22, 1797, at the age of 76. He was a German nobleman and a famous raconteur of tall tales. He joined the Russian military and really did take part in two campaigns against the Ottoman Turks.

The Baron was born in Bodenwerder, Electorate of Brunswick-Lüneburg, into an aristocratic family of the Hanover region. His father's second cousin, Gerlach Adolph von Munchhausen was prime minister under King George III. Munchhausen started as a page to Anthony Ulrich II of Brunswick-Wolfenbüttel, and followed his employer to the Russian Empire during the Russo-Turkish War (1735–1739). In 1739, he was appointed a cornet in a Russian cavalry regiment named the "Brunswick-Cuirassiers". He was later promoted to rank of lieutenant. He was stationed in Riga, but participated in two campaigns against the Turks in 1740 and 1741. In 1744, he married Jacobine von Dunten and was promoted to Rittmeister, a cavalry captain, in 1750. In 1760 Munchhausen retired to his manor and estates in Bodenwerder, where he lived with his wife until her death in 1790. Munchhausen married a second time to Bernardine von Brunn in 1794. He was 74 and she was 17 at the time of the marriage and it soon ended in divorce. Boros and Brubaker (1996) wrote, "It is said that on their wedding night, the baron retired early, and his bride spent the night dancing with another". In 1795, Bernardine gave birth to a son. Boros and Brubaker (1996) reported that following the birth of this child, it was whispered that 'the life of the Munchausen child will likely be short'. The boy, named Polle, died at approximately 1 year of age under "suspicious circumstances." This author has not seen any elaboration on what those suspicious circumstances were under which young Polle died. Whonamedit.com stated "This marriage was an unhappy one which constantly drove him to debt and caused scandals." However, they did not elaborate on the scandals. Kraus (1886) erroneously reported he did not have any children.

After he returned from the military he developed a reputation as a storyteller, developing witty and highly exaggerated accounts of his adventures in Russia. At the same time, Munchhausen was considered an honest man in business affairs. As one contemporary put it, Munchhausen's unbelievable narratives were designed not to deceive, but "to ridicule the disposition for the marvelous which he observed in some of his acquaintances". (Kareem, 2012)

The fictionalization of Munchhausen began in 1781 through 1783, when seventeen tall tales attributed to him appeared in the eighth and ninth volumes of the Vademecum fur lustige Leute. The internet website Whonamedit.com said the man who created the Munchhausen myth was "a family friend, a penniless scholar and librarian professor" from Kassel, Rudolf Erich Raspe (1737-1794), who allegedly "had had to flee England because of thefts". Several sources state the majority of the stories Rapse wrote about were based on folktales that have been in circulation for many centuries before Munchhausen's birth. Fisher (2006) reported the real-life Baron Munchhausen was said to be deeply annoyed that his name had been dragged into public consciousness as the Lügenbaron (German: "Baron of Lies") through the publication of stories under his name. One author (Gross, 2008) support Munchausen's historic complaint because Munchausen was not ever openly accused of nor confirmed to have intentionally injured himself, his own or other children. His picture is below:

From http://en.wikipedia.org/wiki/Baron_M%C3%BCnchhausen#mediaviewer/File:Bruckner_-_M%C3%BCnchhausen.jpg.

His Myths

Some of the fantastic tales of the Baron von Munchausen reported by Raspe (2007 edition) were the following:

In Chapter II he wrote of the Baron: "Night and darkness overtook me. No village was to be seen. The country was covered with snow, and I was unacquainted with the road.

Tired, I alighted, and fastened my horse to something like a pointed stump of a tree, which appeared above the snow; for the sake of safety I placed my pistols under my arm, and laid down on the snow, where I slept so soundly that I did not open my eyes till full daylight. It is not easy to conceive my astonishment to find myself in the midst of a village, lying in a churchyard; nor was my horse to be seen, but I heard him soon after neigh somewhere above me. On looking upwards I beheld him hanging by his bridle of the weather-cock of the steeple. Matters were now very plain to me: the village had been covered with snow overnight; a sudden change of weather had taken place; I had sunk down to the churchyard while asleep, gently, and in the same proportion as the snow had melted away; and what in the dark I had taken to be a stump of a little tree appearing above the snow, to which I had tied my hose, proved to have been the cross or weather-cock of the steeple!"

In that same tale, the Baron said "in the midst of a dreary forest I spied a terrible wolf making after me, with all the speed of a ravenous winter hunger. He soon overtook me. There was no possibility of escape. Mechanically I laid myself down flat in the sledge, and let my horse run for our safety. What I wished, but hardly hoped or expected, happened immediately after. The wolf did not mind me in the least, but took a leap over me, and falling furiously on the house, began instantly to tear and devour the hind-part of the poor animal, which ran the faster for his pain and terror. Thus unnoticed and safe myself, I lifted my head slyly up, and with horror I behold that the wolf had ate his way into the horse's body; it was not long before he had fairly forced himself into it, when I took my advantage, and fell upon him with the butt-end of my whip. This unexpected attack in his rear frightened him so much, that he leaped forward with all his might: the horse's carcase dropped on the ground, but in his place the wolf was in the harness, and I on my part whipping him continually; we both arrived in full career safe at St. Petersburg, contrary to our respective expectations, and very much to the astonishment of the spectators."

In Chapter IV he wrote, "The fiercest and most dangerous animals generally came upon me when defenceless, as if they had a notion or an instinctive intimation of it. Thus a frightful wolf rushed me upon so suddenly, and so close, that I could do nothing but follow mechanical instinct, and thrust my fist into his open mouth. For safety's sake I pushed on and on, till my arm was fairly in up to the shoulder. How should I disengage myself? I was not much pleased with my awkward situation—with a wolf face to face; our ogling was not of the most pleasant kind. If I withdrew my arm, then the animal would fly the more furiously upon me; that I saw in his flaming eyes. In short, I laid hold of his tail, turned him inside out like a glove, and flung him to the ground, where I left him."

In Chapter V he reported on his exploits with his favorite, female, greyhound hunting dog, "I never had or saw a better. She grew old in my service, and was not remarkable for her size, but rather for her uncommon swiftness. I always coursed with her. Had you seen her you must have admired her, and would not have wondered at my predilection, and at my coursing her so much. She ran so fast, so much, and so long in my service that she actually ran off her legs; so that, in the latter part of her life, I was under the necessity of working and using her only as a terrier, in which quality she still served me many years.

Coursing one day a hare, which appeared to me uncommonly big, I pitied my poor bitch, being big with pups, yet she would course as fast as ever. I could follow her on horseback only at a great distance. At once I heard a cry as it were a pack of hounds—but so weak and faint that I hardly knew what to make of it. Coming up to them I was greatly surprised. The hare had littered in running; the same had happened to my bitch in coursing, and there were just as many leverets as pups. By instinct the former ran, the latter coursed; and thus I found myself in possession at once of six hares and as many dogs, at the end of a course which had only begun with one."

And finally for this writing's purposes, Raspe wrote in Chapter VI, "I was not always successful. I had the misfortune to be overpowered by numbers, to be made prisoner of war; and, what is worse, but always usual among the Turks, to be sold for a slave. [The Baron was afterwards in great favour with the Grand Seignior, as will appear hereafter.] In that state of humiliation, my daily task was not very hard and laborious, but rather singular and irksome. It was to drive the Sultan's bees every morning to their pasture-grounds, to attend them all the day long, and against night to drive them back to their hives. One evening I missed a bee, and soon observed that two bears had fallen upon her to tear her to pieces for the honey she carried. I had nothing like an offensive weapon in my hands but the silver hatchet, which is the badge of the Sultan's gardeners and farmers. I threw it at the robbers, with an intention to frightening them away, and set the poor bee at liberty; but, by an unlucky turn of my arm, it flew upwards and continued rising till it reached the moon. How should I recover it? How fetch it down again? I recollected that Turkey-beans grow very quick, and run up to an astonishing height. I planted one immediately; it grew, and actually fastened itself to one of the moon's horns. I had no more to do now but to climb up by it into the moon where I safely arrived, and had a troublesome piece of business before I could find my silver hatchet, in a place where everything has the brightness of silver; at least, however, I found it in a heap of chaff and chopped straw. I was not for returning; but, alas! The heat of the sun had dried up my bean; it was totally useless for my descent; so I fell to work, and twisted me a rope of that chopped straw, as long and as well as I could make it. This I fastened to one of the moon's horns, and slid down to the end of it."

There are many more tales of the alleged adventures of Baron von Munchausen told by Raspe. These include Baron von Munchausen riding into battle on a cannonball and pulling himself up by his bootstraps. As fun and fantastic as these tales appear to the audience in Munchausen's time and ours, the writer (Raspe) repeatedly commented in these stories on how honest Munchausen was known to be in his day and time. This propensity for others to mimic his tall tales and invent their own persists to this day and time. Unfortunately, some of those tales involve unlikely sources of injuries to the story teller's own body (currently called Factitious Disorder Imposed on Self). Some of those tales also involve unlikely and untrue sources of injuries to children's' bodies (currently called Factitious Disorder Imposed on Others). The following sections will discuss these two processes.

Factitious Disorder Imposed on Self

(Munchausen Syndrome-MS)

Factitious Disorder Imposed on Self (Munchausen's Syndrome-MS) involves falsification or induction of physical and/or psychological injury on oneself even in the absence of obvious external rewards without better explanation by another mental disorder.

In regards to physical self-injury, one source reported the most famous case to be William McIlhoy who made it into Guinness World Records "but he didn't have many fans at Britain's National Hospital Service. After 400 operations in 100 different hospitals, McIlhoy ran up $4 million worth of medical bills. The famous Munchausen syndrome sufferer died in a retirement home in 1983". (howstuffwork.com).

Another source (Time Magazine, 1979) reported on a Stewart McIroy from Ireland but all other information about Mr. McIroy is satisfactorily similar to conclude he is the same person as the abovementioned William McIilhoy. The entire Time magazine article is printed below to show the extreme lengths Mr. McIlhoy (and others) will go to satisfy their urge for self-harm and attention. The article stated:

"Stewart McIlroy may or may not have been born around 1915 in County Donegal, Ireland. Other facts of his life are equally vague. But to two London doctors who spent four years investigating hospital records in the British Isles, one thing about McIlroy is certain: he is an incurable hospital addict. In the past 34 years he has been admitted at least 207 times to 68 different hospitals in Ireland, England, Scotland and Wales for a breathtaking variety of diseases and disorders. Indeed, McIlroy seems beyond doubt to be the all-time champion sufferer of Munchausen's syndrome.

Those afflicted with the syndrome (named after Baron Munchhausen, an 18th century raconteur whose tales of adventure made his name synonymous with exaggeration) are driven to immerse themselves in hospital dramas. With a combination of medical knowledge and dramatic flair, victims produce or fake symptoms so skillfully that they are admitted to hospitals, treated and often operated on for nonexistent disorders.

Tracing McIlroy's hospital visits was obviously a labor of love for Neurologist C.A. Pallis of Hammersmith Hospital and Rheumatologist A.N. Bamji of Middlesex Hospital. In their report to the British Medical Journal, they meticulously listed the 22 surnames and eight first names used in various combinations by McIlroy in registering at different hospitals. (McIlroy was identified by the description in clinical records of his scars and other physical characteristics.) The names of all the hospitals and the number of admittances to each were also faithfully recorded.

McIlroy's ruses worked in part because he had a real disability, a neurological disorder that affected his upper torso and arms and conceivably could have spread to other parts of his body. That made it easy for him to feign numbness wherever and whenever he chose. But he also could use medical jargon to describe the symptoms he could fake so well. When he suffered his frequent temporary losses of speech, he compensated by writing a technical account of his medical and personal history. These invariably included the fact that all his relatives had met violent deaths at the hands of I.R.A. "bombers and gunmen"--which made it difficult for anyone to check on his real identity.

McIlroy suffered mightily over the years to satisfy his addiction. He was subjected to thousands of X rays and blood tests; his abdomen was crisscrossed with scars where doctors made incisions during exploratory operations. His spine was punctured 48 times to get spinal fluid in order to check for evidence of cranial hemorrhaging or spinal disorders. "How much Mr. McIlroy cost the health services," the doctors wrote, "will remain a matter for conjecture. The sum must run into six, possibly seven figures."

After checking into Belfast City Hospital in 1976 for one of his few legitimate visits (he had fallen and fractured his right leg), McIlroy made a few brief appearances at other hospitals and then disappeared for more than a year. The two investigators assumed that he had died. But he resurfaced at a Birmingham nursing home last June, then at hospitals in Ireland and Scotland, and was discharged from another one in London as recently as August. Diagnosis: McIlroy is alive--and still ailing--in the British Isles."

This author has worked with very few patients with confirmed intentional infliction of physical damage to their body. All of those encounters were very brief due to the patient's choices. The first case involved a Caucasian male in his mid-50s at the time of the assessment. He was remarkable in that he had a pseudoseizure and spasmed on the waiting room floor (but did not have any loss of bladder control) before the assessment session even commenced. Other mental health-care staff at that clinic knew him from other clinics and said he was known for these pseudoseizures. His back medical history included approximately 70 operations and/or medical procedures for many cysts and blisters. Physicians eventually got suspicious and cultured the material in the pus pockets and found them filled with the man's urine and feces. The man had injected every part of his body he could reach, including his testicles, with his urine and feces. His testicles had been so severely infected he eventually had to have them both removed. He was married with two children at the time of our first session. His wife and the children were with him during his first session. He and they never returned for additional sessions.

The second case was a Caucasian female in her mid-40s. She had a self-realization even as a young child (pre-teen) that her first contact with medical personnel was filled with something very nice that she had never experienced before: human compassion. Her first injury was innocent due to an accidental bone break. However, she then began intentionally injuring herself severely enough that she needed additional medical attention. These self-injuries included jumping out of progressively higher trees (until she broke something) and pounding on her feet with a hammer until more bones broke, necessitating additional medical attention. Her insight into her self-harm behavior did not prevent her from doing Munchausen by Proxy on her four children, even to the point one of them died. She had her children repeatedly removed from her care and custody by the courts and never got her first four back. She steadfastly denied significantly neglecting or abusing them and steadfastly refused counseling or therapy.

Most people doing Munchausen Syndrome behaviors are extremely unhappy people and it is difficult for most readers to read about their self-damaging behaviors. However, in order for the reader (especially clinicians) to fully understand the depths of self-damage that these people commit, I mention the most extreme cases I have encountered (above) and refer them to see the article and pictures published by Lin et al. (2012) of the young man who completely destroyed both of his eyes through self-injury over a period of one year. His explanations for his severe, vision-destroying injuries to each eye were "a cat scratched it" and "he was in the bathroom and it just exploded". He denied the entire time that he was injuring himself. I defer on publishing those pictures here due to their extremely high potential to disturb most readers. I mention these extremes solely to alert the reader of the great potential for physical damage that exists in some of these people should the reader encounter one (suspected or confirmed).

In regards to male/female balance, Metha and Kahn (2002) reported that 93% of the MS patients on cardiac wards who were diagnosed as Munchausen's Syndrome were males. They did not report the racial composition of the subjects. Papadopalous and Bell (1999) reported on five cases of neurological Factitious Disorder in a London, England, hospital. Four of the five cases were males. All five were recognized by hospital staff for multiple hospitalizations in the past. The races of the subjects were not reported. Gregory and Jindal (2006) reported the male/female ratio of admission and diagnosis of MS was 50/50. The race of their patients was not reported.

What inner dynamics drive people to hurt themselves so badly if they are not motivated for money or other materialist rewards? An article written for the general public ("Munchausen Syndrome" at MedicineNet.com) stated "Although there is no specific cause for Munchausen syndrome, like most other mental disorders, it is understood to be the result of a combination of biological vulnerabilities, ways of thinking, and social stressors (biopsychosocial model). Little is known about the specific biological vulnerabilities from which individuals with Munchausen syndrome are more likely to suffer. Psychologically, sufferers of this mental illness tend to have an increased need for control, an imbalance in the level of self-esteem (either low or excessively high), and a vulnerability to suffering from depression, anxiety, or substance abuse. Personality traits of individuals who have a history of feigning or inducing symptoms in themselves include some that are in common with borderline personality disorder (for example, if the person is dissociative or has another disturbance in their identity/sense of self; unstable relationships, recurrent self-mutilation, and/or recurrent thoughts or attempts at suicide) or antisocial personality disorder (for example, a tendency to lie, disregard the safety of themselves or others, and to have little empathy for others). Risk factors for people with Munchausen syndrome include enduring a major negative event (trauma) during their own childhood (such as a serious illness of themselves, a close family member or friend), having a grudge against the medical profession or having been themselves the victim of neglect, physical or sexual abuse, or other forms of maltreatment during childhood." This article suffers from describing many general symptoms that occur in many other disorders so none of the factors it mentions are truly explanatory or causative of Munchausen Syndrome alone.

Do psychological tests reveal anything more specific about these people? This author was not able to test the male of the above-mentioned MS pair he encountered. Swain (1981) did IQ testing and personality testing with a 28-year-old female who was self-harming. He reported she had an above-average IQ (121). He also did Thematic Apperception Test and Rorschach testing. He concluded her performances indicated she was "generally rebellious against authority figures". Eisendrath & McNeil (2002) and Gregory (2006) reported "fake bad" profile with elevations across all the subscales of the Minnesota Multiphasic Personality Inventory (MMPI). This verifies that people in this category of psychopathology have mathematically-significant high need to feign illness or problems. These elevated MMPI fake bad (Lie) validity scale suggests severe psychopathology in and of itself but can occur in many other different diagnostic categories.

This author has evaluated eleven adult and teenage children who would fall into the Munchausen Syndrome category. They were all guilty of fabricating wildly improbable tales about their exploits and/or their physical problems. However, *none* of them had done any of the horrendous physical damage to their bodies discussed in the most of the cases above or in other cited sources. Therefore, their test results are probably not as extreme as those who do severe damage to themselves or others and these data would not be generalizable to other, more extreme cases. The people this author tested ranged in age from 16 to 46. All were adult except for two teenage females. All were Caucasian. Seven of the 11 were females. All were administered a standard battery of psychological tests: the Kaufman Brief Intelligence Test (KBIT), Millon Personality Tests (Millon Clinical Multiaxial Inventory-III or Millon Adolescent Clinical Inventory), the Bender-Gestalt Visual-Motor test and a Trauma Inventory. The quantifiable tests (KBIT, Millon and Bender) obtained the following results:

On intelligence, all had fairly average IQ scores on the KBIT. None of their IQs were in the bottom 5% and none were in the top 10%. They appeared smart enough to concoct the stories but not smart enough to realize their stories would be investigated for veracity.

In regards to psychopathology, three of them had the Millon validity scale titled "Desirability" significantly elevated. This validity scale detects people excessively denying any minor problems or faults that all of us have and most of us admit. This pathological denial would be expected in this population since they are denying their fabrication while recounting expanded, extended or excessively fantastic stories about themselves or their children while denying they are fabricating.

The failure of these and other personality tests to correlate highly with MS does not occur only to MS. Personality tests frequently fail to correlate highly with any specific behavior due to the significant overlap of symptoms between diagnostic categories that is described as "polythetic" by all of the DSMs. This term (polythetic) means there are many (poly) theses (thetic) for the source of any one symptom.   This symptom overlap is crucial for understating many of the personality disorders. An EBSCOhost search of the terms "borderline- sexual-abuse" identified

33 studies examining the relationship of sexual abuse and Borderline Personality Disorder. Many personality-disordered people are victims of severe and chronic abuse. Self-abuse is often an adult sequellae of childhood abuse. Munchausen Syndrome needs to be considered a form of self-abuse.

Another problem with trying to find "the" personality of a MS person is that "personality" is a rather broad term and many personality test results only correlate around .30 with any real-world behaviors. That is because personality tests often measured multi-faceted components (e.g., the MMPI has ten clinical subscales, the MCMI has 21 and so on). The underling consistency across all MS clients is they fake an illness (physical or mental) to get internal rewards.

In regards to organicity, none of them showed any signs of organicity or diffuse brain damage on the Bender-Gestalt but one had a history of seizures and one of them had a significant childhood brain injury.

The lack of other published test results on people with confirmed or suspected MS speaks more to the evasiveness and manipulativeness of these people than of the disinterest, carelessness or incompetence of the health care professions. Many case histories on people with MS end with the patient refusing to get psychiatric help or simply walking out the facility door against medical advice (AMA).

This author hypothesizes that the personality or psychopathology of the MS patient would vary according to the amount of self-harm done. For example, someone who merely repeatedly caused skin rashes would have less serious psychopathology than one who completely disfigured or maimed themselves. This range of self-harm would suggest the range of pathological motivation ranges from simply "too needy of attention" to "severe self-hatred". However, the rarity of the MS phenomenon in combination with the evasiveness and elusiveness of the individual once they are detected makes full, deeper understanding of their psychopathology difficult to assess and understand. While various authors calculate epidemiology to be around 0.03% of a neurology data base sample (Bauer and Boegner, 1996) to 0.08% (Sutherland & Rodin, 1990) of a general hospital, the true incidence will never be known. While many theorize the underlying diagnosis of a MS person ranges from neurotic to psychotic, schizophrenic and psychopathic, the "true" diagnosis can be as radical as Dissociative Identity Disorder (DID). For example, this author had one case of a person with DID who developed psychogenic paralysis of one hand when traumatic memories were trying to surface to consciousness. The paralysis persisted out of the therapy office and some of the patient's alter egos eventually sought help for her hand dysfunction from a neurologist who diagnosed the problem as carpel tunnel syndrome. He did the traditional carpel tunnel operative procedures with apparent success but one of the alternate, little child personalities of the DID who did not know about the operation kept awakening in the middle of sleep to find the bandages and stitches, kept panicking and removing the stitches from the operative site, repeatedly leaving a bloody mess that the "host" or other personalities would have to deal with. The little child was confused, angry and terrified of the stitches so she took them out. This necessitated repeated re-suture of the site but the person eventually needed to go to different emergency rooms in different towns so she her extreme psychopathology would not get detected. Her case would superficially appear to be self-harm for attention but the full dynamics were much deeper.

So what internal reward do they seem to seek? Affection. Caring. Attention. Love.

One MS person stated something like, "I don't feel the pain; I just feel the love" (source unavailable). We all receive comfort and attention from caretakers when we are physically or mentally ill. That is part of the caregiver/patient dyad. It is the extreme extent that the MS people go to receive the love and caring that is pathological. It is extreme in the extent they will injure their bodies. It is extreme in the extent they will go to cover it up (direct lying, assuming false identities, visiting many different facilities). It is extreme to the extent of the persistence and chronicity they display in seeking the love.

Another person named Avigal, a survivor of MS, wrote the following about her childhood filled with abuse and terror: "When I was five years old, my father began to abuse me sexually. In response, I withdrew and detached myself from my family. In my frightening life, I was forced to focus on survival, so I hid. There was a huge walk-in closet in my bedroom, cluttered with large plastic bags filled with clothes. I spent hours at a time, day after day, hiding in that closet with the bags on top of me. I assured myself that if an intruder opened the door and peeked in, he would see only bags, shoes and clothes. I would be invisible. My closet soon became my refuge. I spent days in darkness and silence, clutching my doll close to my body, *fantasizing about being loved.*" (Avigal & Hall, 2012, page 1). The most severely abused people experience the most intense emotions and act out those feelings most drastically. Sometimes they act these feelings out on themselves. Sometimes they act them out on other people.

Factitious Disorder Imposed on Others

(Munchausen by Proxy-MbP)

Seriously and repeatedly producing intentional harm to one's own body as with Munchausen Syndrome is a perplexing, disturbing and sometimes deadly process. Seriously and repeatedly injuring a child for one's own purposes is also an extreme, sometimes deadly process. The data on MbP are more voluminous and clearer than the data on MS, possibly due to the higher ability of the educational, medical and child-protective-services systems to monitor and enforce mandates and medical appointments for the child since the child-victim has mandated protection by law in all states in America.

In regards to the victim, Concepcion et al. (2008) reported that most victims of MbP are five years of age or under with average age being 20 months. Half of them were assaulted by poisoning (anticonvulsants or opiates) or suffocation. They also reported there was an 8-10% morbidity rate in the victims. The child's mother was the perpetrator 85% of the time.

In regards to the perpetrator, one must wonder what dynamics are operating in a person who has birthed a child and is supposed to be that child's primary caretaker but functions as its main or sole persecutor and abuser. Libow and Schreier (1986) postulated three categories of MbP: 1) The Help Seekers, 2) The Doctor Addict and 3) the Active Inducers.

Libow and Schrier described the Help Seeker as "taking her children to be seen less persistently over time or for only one single episode of factitious complaints. This is because the mother's medical-attention seeking represents different needs: rather than serving to fuel and re-enact long-term transference issues, a medical confrontation with these patients often helps a mother communicate such problems as her anxiety, exhaustion, or depression." This appears to be an "assistance seeking" process.

In regards to the Doctor Addicts, Libow and Schrier stated "the falsifications were more passive. These mothers were personally convinced that their children were ill, despite repeated tests and examinations which showed the contrary, and their use of deception did not extend past false history of reporting of history and symptoms." Somewhat contradictorily, they later described the Doctor Addict MbP mother as "distrustful" and "angry", but they postulated that anger might be possibly due to a fear of exposure.

In contrast, Libow and Schrier described the Active Inducer as having "a maternal style above suspicion; almost all of the mothers have been described as cooperative, concerned, loving, devoted, and trustworthy; many are nurses or other kinds of health care professionals. Their child victims are usually infants or preschool children who are too young to resist or serve as informants in the unraveling of their mysterious illnesses."

It is probable that these three subtypes have different personality dynamics since the last one (The Inducer) is much more of an active aggressor toward the child and the other two (The Help Seeker and Doctor Addict) seem more passive, usually merely withholding treatment or falsifying illness to continue the child's illness for her purposes. However, this author believes it is also crucial to emphasize the difference between any of these subcategories and those caregivers who do behaviors that endanger or end the child's life, not merely sicken it. This author believes the personality of an MbP perpetrator who allows or causes their child to get fatally sick is different from other MbP perpetrators who produce only chronic, mild dysfunction or disease in their child or misreport symptoms or history. The perpetrator's serious lack of consideration of the child's right to life is another level of psychopathology and they should be assessed and treated differently, with much greater concern for the victim's rights and much more intense assessment of the perpetrator's causes of this level of hatred and/or inconsideration (dehumanization) of their victim.

Although many studies and surveys report a female is the usual perpetrator in a vast majority of cases, Meadow (1977) reported on fifteen males who were confirmed MbP perpetrators. His data indicated nine of them used smothering in combination with other methods. He also reported five of the fifteen had done MS on themselves in their younger years. Eight of the fifteen had significant histories of somatization disorder and/or fabrication in their own pasts.

Meadow said these data are consistent with female MbP in the occurrence of self-harm (MS), somatization and fabrication of illness in their lives before committing MbP on others. Meadows ominously reported that these men's self-harm behaviors went into abeyance when they were injuring the children and then returned when the child got healthy or died. Similar to data about some female MbP perpetrators, these male perpetrators were described as "overdemanding, overbearing, and unreasonable." Even those who initially seemed to behave reasonably were soon found to lose their temper easily and become irritated with staff. These fathers or father-surrogates were quick to make formal complaints and to seek legal redress for the perceived failure of the health care system to provide either satisfactory service or care for their child. Five families, at the instigation of the father, were involved in formal litigation against a hospital." Incidentally, Meadow reported that there were repeated suspicious fires in several of these perpetrators' houses and a high incidence of animal fatalities of suspicious nature in their houses. One can only speculate about the sources of these men's extreme anger since Meadow did not assess their childhood background for the usual factors associated with extreme emotional lability (abuse, neglect or head injury). Below is a list of some of the improbable or disproven claims those male perpetrators made about their own special accomplishments:

- South of England sailing champion.
- Amateur Athletic Association junior champion, 800 metres.
- Fighting alongside Prince Andrew in the Falklands war; showing photograph of Fleet Air Arm passing out parade, claiming to identify himself.
- Academic achievement—nine GCSE grades, mainly A and B" (but the school head confirmed that on the first day of exams he turned up at school with his arm in a sling, "unable to write," and had achieved no grades).
- Devised poster campaign for national election victory, also invented British Telecom TV advertisement.
- Writer of two novels, one of which has been adapted for film.
- Writing screenplay for film. He spent much time on the telephone at home speaking to Steven (Spielberg), convincing his wife to the extent that she agreed to dress up in her best clothes to accompany him to the studio to meet the cast—but "the chauffeur driven Rolls Royce broke down" on the way to their house.
- Manager of transport depot supervising 58 employees.
- Senior security position for prestigious London office block-home events.

The reader will note the similarities of these improbable claims to the improbable claims of the malingerers this author detailed in the first section of this article. Manipulation to attain external reward does not seem to be much different to this author from manipulation to attain internal reward and there are probably both internal and external types of rewards in most manipulations.

There is very little published research on the personality or other psychological factors regarding the perpetrators of MbP. Concepcion and Garcia (1999) did administer the Rorschach Projective cards to one 50-year-old female who repeatedly brought her 13-year-old son to the hospital with complaints of blood in his urine. The blood disappeared from his urine any time the hospital staff were the ones taking the urine sample and the mother's history included (1) previous history of frequent admissions in other hospitals, (2) voluntary discharge against medical advice (AMA) and abandon of former treatments, (3) several formal complaints against medical staff for malpractice, and (4) previous demands for mental care attention for family members without continuity of treatment in any case.

They interpreted her Rorschach results to indicate "she had a pessimistic view of her environment (MOR↑), a low conventionality (X +%↓, P↓), and a marked cognitive rigidity (a:p). The mother is avoidant and uncomplex and she biases her perception according to her needs. She had an evitative (avoidant) style toward the affective stimuli, with a low recording capacity for inner discomfort and low emotional interchanges. She can maintain a superficially adaptative behavior, but only after limiting her resources and relationships." These authors concluded she suffered from a personality disorder, but given there are 10 different personality disorders listed in the current DSM-5 that are widely divergent in their manifestations, Concepcion and Garcia's personality disorder diagnosis lacks adequate specificity.

This author has also tested four adults who were diagnosed with Munchausen by Proxy with the same test battery described above for MS people. None of them were guilty of inflicting horrendous physical damage described above and in other sources. Three of them had convinced their child that their other parent had physically and/or sexually abused them. The other one was the mid-40s female described in an earlier section of this paper who had lost one child by death via medical neglect and repeatedly lost legal custody of all of the others.

They were three females, one male. They were all Caucasians.

In regards to intelligence scores, all of them but one had average scores (between 85 and 115).

In regards to psychopathology, three of the four had elevated Desirability validity scales on the MCMI-III. These elevated "fake good" results are congruent with their denial of misbehaviors when they are suspected of or caught doing harm to others. Two of the four had significantly elevated Histrionic Personality Disorder scales.

In regards to organicity, none of them had any glaring indicators of brain damage on the Bender-Gestalts.

This author's test data also showed no major intellectual deficits in these people. They showed an interesting pattern of psychopathology in terms of repeated, excessive denial that they also exhibited in many other venues when being questioned about their children's medical concerns. Their MCMI responses showed major tendencies of having Histrionic Personality Disorder. The DSM-5 describes the Histrionic as being "uncomfortable when they are not the center of attention, being inappropriately seductive or provocative, having rapidly shifting and shallow expressions of emotions, using physical appearance to draw attention to oneself, speaking excessively impressionistic, being self-dramatizing and theatrical, being easily influenced by others and considering relationships to be more intimate than they really are" (p. 326). Many of these symptoms are quite frequently found in describing the caretakers who commit Munchausen by Proxy. These tests results are congruent with their inappropriate attention-seeking activities surrounding their children's health problems. They consistently present themselves more much more intimate in their relationship with their victims than they really are. However, one must again note that not all people with Histrionic Personality Disorder commit Munchausen by Proxy.

Many investigators in this field focus more on detection than diagnosis since a) so little psychological testing has been done, b) that which has been done (including this author's) would lead to many "false positive" diagnoses if one merely relies on the test results and c) other behavior patterns are also prone to many false positives. Chiczewski and Kelly (2003) recommended medical personnel be on the lookout for the following behavior patterns:

1) The child's described medical problem does not respond to the normal course of treatment.
2) There are multiple admissions of the same child to the same facility with similar complaints or a variety of illnesses.
3) There is a family history of similar incidents with siblings, including multiple SIDS (sudden infant syndrome) in siblings.
4) Signs and symptoms disappear upon the removal of the child from its parent(s).
5) The caregiver attempts to convince the medical staff of illness without any signs (including laboratory results) or symptoms.

Many authors also described the perpetrator as a) often having worked in the medical field, b) done child care, c) being over-knowledgeable of diseases and d) behaving more as a consultant to the child than as a parent. However, one must be cautious about the latter factors (c and d) because the "good" parent of a child suffering real chronic, unremitting physical illness will be active in the child's treatment and will want to learn from medical staff and provide what knowledge they have to the treatment teams. The crucial deficits in MbP caregivers are that they do not follow up on the child's proposed medical treatments after the child is discharged to their care and the child repeatedly relapses into illness when in their care. The other caveat (again) is that none of these factors (1-5 or a-d) in isolation or in combination automatically proves MbP is being performed.

Sometimes the general parameters listed above proved inadequate and professionals considered or conducted secret surveillance of the mother and child in a special hospital unit. Beckwood-Ball

(2000) objected to covert surveillance as an "invasion of privacy" but many hospital units have resorted to it. This author has heard of it being used in Cleveland, Ohio, hospitals since the 1970s but cannot find studies that far back. Vaught & Fleetwood (2002) and Hall et al. (2000) reported the use of and results of covert video monitoring of the mother/child interactions in the hospital since 1993 (facility names and locations not reported). Vaught and Fleetwood reported on one case of covert video surveillance (CVS) and stated the hospital staff covertly observed the child's mother inject something from a syringe into her child's IV line and then attempt to suffocate her with a pillow. Hall et al. (2000) reported "A diagnosis of MSBP was made in 23 of 41 patients monitored. CVS was required to make the diagnosis in 13 (56.1%) of these 23, and supportive of the diagnosis in 5 (21.7%) cases. On a positive note, in 4 patients this surveillance was instrumental in establishing innocence of the parents." MSBP was more common in Caucasian patients than in other ethnic groups seen at their hospital. Fifty-five percent of mothers gave a history of health care work or study and another 25% had previously worked in day-care. They stated, "Although many of caretakers fit the profile of MSBP such as excessive familiarity with medical staff, eagerness for invasive medical testing, and history of health care work, these characteristics were *not sensitive indicators (italics added by this author)* of MSBP in our study. Even when present, they were not sufficiently compelling to make the diagnosis." The words "not sensitive indicators" also means there would be many false positives if only these criteria were used. In addition, in all cases, the person who induced, fabricated, or staged the illness was the mother and the average time of CVS needed until discovery of the intentional injury was around three days. This report also revealed another example of the MbP perpetrator's pathology: the unit recorded the telephone conversations of some of the mother's telephone conversations on the hospital telephone in the patient's room or nurse's station. They noted that the mother told lies on the phone about the child's condition and diagnosis even as the child was in the hospital bed.

In another forensic technique, Wenk (2003) reported that DNA analysis was done on a child's pus and established that the components of the pus were actually from the child's mother's body.

This author has experienced many cases and hearings around the issue of MbP. The courts in these cases seemed to be satisfied enough with findings that the suspected caregiver had told documented untruths about the child and had not followed upon recommended treatment or diagnoses of the child (mental and/or physical) to take the legal custody of the child away from the parent. This author was unable to get long-term feedback as to whether the parent ever regained unsupervised visitation with the child or had their parental rights terminated.

This author observed another example of the desperation of the MbP perpetrator to sustain the fantasy of others alleged abuse of their child in a forensic case. The case initially came to me because people suspected the mother was filling her child's young mind with false information regarding the child's father sexually abusing the child. This writer did an evaluation of the mother, father and child and concluded the mother was spuriously distorting the child's memories and relationship with the father. This conclusion was heavily based on, among other things, the child using words to describe her alleged sexual interactions with her father that a child of her age would never normally use. In addition, she was alleging these attacks occurred at times that did not match the real situation in the house. The father was awarded custody of the child on the basis all the information, including my reports. However, when the mother got unsupervised time with the child the mother secretly took the child to five other psychologists or counselors for the alleged purpose of further "sexual assault" assessment. The father then sued for sole legal and physical custody of the child and this author was subpoenaed to testify regarding custody matters.

The writer heard no other witnesses' testimony as is typical in court proceedings and only found out the judge's decision in the father's favor several weeks later when the father called. He said that the judge seemed to perceive the custody case as a typical child-custody case in spite of my report until the mother got on the stand and started making many new, bizarre, false allegations of sexual abuse against her husband. This behavior was extremely inappropriate since all allegations were supposed to have been declared and investigated prior to the trial. The mother could not contain her pathological need to make false allegations and it cost her credibility, legal custody of her child and unsupervised visitation with her child.

Etiological Considerations

The potential etiology (cause) of these severe behaviors can range across all theories of human psychopathology from the deepest Freudian psychoanalytic theory to the most superficial behavioral, black-box approach to anything in between. Any considerations of transference and unconscious processes as motivators for these misbehaviors stem from the Freudian perspective while any rewards (internal or external) the person derives from the injuries to self or others is fully understandable from an operant conditioning paradigm of B.F. Skinner. This author has also dealt with several cases where the MbP perpetrator was taken to many doctors for supposed physical problems when they were children. That would make the pathological MbP misbehavior a product of modeling (Vicarious Reinforcement) as described by Bandura (1977).

Robbins (1991) mentioned the relevance of Family Systems Theory, Theories of Women's Psychological Development and Child Abuse Theory for understanding the dynamics of Munchausen (MS) and MbP behaviors. Robbins said the Family Systems Theory approach would help understand the role the child's alleged or inflicted sickness played in the family dynamics. Many mother/child MbP relationships have described the mother as "overinvolved and enmeshed" but with the child fulfilling some of the mother's needs that are subverted in her marriage (Masters, Dunsworth and Williams, 1988).

Women's Psychological Development Theory state that women get their primary identity based on connection to and caring for others as compared to men's identity achieved through competition and separation (Gilligan, 1982, and others). Excessive sacrifice of self-care for the sake of other-care can lead to resentment, frustration, feelings of deprivation and depression. Leeder (1990) reported that mothers with MbP expressed significant dissatisfaction with the "traditional" mothering role. This makes the child vulnerable to abuse and/or neglect out of conscious or unconscious anger at the child.

Child abuse theory is relevant in understanding MS and MbP due to the higher ratio of female sexual abuse victims than male sexual abuse victims across decades of research on the incidence of child sexual abuse. While most estimates of female child sexual abuse hover around 25% by the time they are 18, a lesser proportion (1/9) males are estimated to be sexually abused by the time they are 18. Many authors (e.g., Cramer, Gershberg & Stern, 1971) reported that mothers doing MbP report significant emotional, sexual and/or physical abuse in their childhoods. Bools, Neale, and Meadow (1994) studied 47 mothers who had conducted MbP by smothering and poisoning their children as part of their fabrications. When these mothers' lifetime psychiatric histories were collected, previous factitious or somatoform disorders, self-harm, and/or alcohol-drug misuse appeared in all of them. The most notable psychopathology found was the presence of a personality disorder in 17 mothers, predominantly histrionic and borderline types.

While most clinicians focus on "the diagnosis" of these abuse victims/MbP perpetrators, this author would like to emphasize the enormous and excessive emotionality that severe physical and sexual abuse create in the victims and the result the abuses produce: Post Traumatic Stress Disorder (PTSD). This author strongly encourages all therapists working with severe and chronic mental disorders to assess for physical abuse, sexual abuse and abandonment experiences in every patient/client they work with, MS, MbP or not. Avigal and Hall (2012) wrote a book on their therapy case of severe Munchausen Syndrome that took over four years to resolve. She (Avigal) reported a childhood history full of physical and sexual abused to herself, domestic violence by her father against her mother and great guilt that she could not fix the family. While one case history does not make a law, the clinical studies reviewed for this article are replete with cases of MS that reported severe abuse, neglect and childhood family chaos.

Therapy

Once one has a correct and thorough understanding of the diagnosis, etiology and dynamics of each MS or MbP person, effective therapy can begin. Treatment must be individualized for each perpetrator.

The assessment and treatment of the victim/alleged victim can follow any standard protocols for victim-therapy such as the manual *The Courage to Heal* (1994). Special attention must be paid to three factors in working with *young* MbP victims:

1) Always create safety and assure them that they are safe from further victimization. This is superficially achieved by removing the child and assuring them that their perpetrators cannot get to them anymore. However, this rescue is complicated by several factors: a) a young child has no adult meaning of the word "safe" because they are a child; b) the child may always be afraid to be honest with their rescuers about what abuse they really experienced because they never feel completely safe, c) the child may not be safe from

their persecutor forever. The courts have returned many of these children to their perpetrators if there was not adequate legal evidence to remove the child from their custody after follow-up judicial reviews of all evidence.

2) Some perpetrators convince the child that he or she is really sick mentally and/or physically so the child will not report their behaviors as abuse because they do not view it as abuse no matter how often you explain it to them, and

3) Some perpetrators instill terror in their young victims by telling them the perpetrator can spot them no matter where they are with mental telepathy or can come to them in their dreams and psychically hurt them if they ever tell what was done to them. Little children believe these outlandish coercions as much as they believe in Santa Clause, the Easter Bunny or the Tooth Fairy.

Getting the full truth from an adult MS is also very difficult possibly due to some of the factors listed above and others (the secondary gain they get). In addition, some adult MS perpetrators may still be living with or under the control of their victimizers.

Bursten (1965) stated, "We have never successfully treated a person with Munchausen's Syndrome, nor do we know of any person who has." Such a pessimistic statement! Can it be true? Is the prognosis so grim for MS and MbP people as to be incurable? Can Bursten's pessimism be merely due to the limited approaches of the 1960s compared to the treatment options and more advanced understanding of psychopathology we have today? Can it be due to the limits of psychiatry at that time? Can it be due to limiting factors of the therapists? Is it any better today?

Mental health has assuredly made great strides in the understanding of etiology, diagnosis and treatment of these disorders since 1965. However, the cases and research reviewed for this paper indicate there are many, many factors that give these types of cases great difficulty for the successful conduct of therapy and/or case manager. First, many of the case histories reported detail the multi-decades, multi-facility, multi-therapist, multi-deceptions that the most severe MS and MbP patients perform. These factors suggest deeply ingrained, transference-based destructiveness with incredibly manipulative components to attempt to continue the damage to self or child. The manipulativeness in the chronic and severe cases is extremely indicative of a refusal to engage in a therapeutic contract of honest, forthright self-examination and improvement. Comments abound in the case studies reviewed here to the effect that after the person was informed the staff believed their or their children's physical or mental problems were fabricated, the person left the facility, left AMA, walked off, walked away, refused therapy, did not keep their psychiatric appointment, did not pursue therapy, cancelled the appointment and so on. These post-confrontation behaviors all indicate intense avoidance and denial. Schoenfeld et al. (1987) actually wrote that they consider MS to be a form of suicide in that their patient engaged in many self-harm behaviors that could have easily been fatal. Suicide is the ultimate avoidance. His patient told him, "I knew it could be dangerous, but I didn't care. Sometimes I even wanted this (danger). When I didn't die at least I got a few days of peace and quiet." The relief he spoke of was from his feelings of despair and worthlessness associated with factors in his childhood (abuse and neglect). However, these same authors reported the successful treatment of said suicidal-prone MS person with up to a four-year follow-up period.

In addition, Mayo and Haggerty (1984) reported that 10 of 37 cases of Munchausen's were considered to be improved after therapy lasting up to one year. Of those 37 people initially diagnosed with Munchausen's, only 22 had agreed to extensive assessment and/or therapy. While the overall improved rate is around 33%, the higher rate of 50% for those who did participate in any interventions that were offered to them is laudable.

Most authors that did any in-depth evaluation of the MS/MbP patient stated, concluded or reported that there was always multi-diagnosis of the person, not just the Factitious MS or MbP. This would be termed "dual-diagnosis" in the pre-DSM-5 multi-axial diagnostic nomenclature terminology. This author's testing results discussed above substantiates that opinion in most of the cases. Even if the person only had an elevated Desirability validity subscale on the MCMI (or a parallel elevation of the "lie" validity subscale on the MMPI) it was clinically significant in that this pathological denial is at a statistically significant level and has always been related to significant, various pathological behaviors in the real world.

 Some authors suggested using two therapists with these patients. This dual-therapist approach has also been suggested when working with Borderline Personality Disordered patients. This approach provides a "good doctor" who can be purely emotionally supportive and empathetic and a "bad doctor" who is confrontive, inquisitive and analytical. This two-doctor approach would be a limited option in facilities with less homogeneous or numerous staff. Even the consideration of this technique should alert any provider of mental or physical health how difficult and emotionally labile their patients or clients can be. Experience with one of these incredibly labile patient/clients is very stressful for any therapist. They are the cases that therapists usually tell "battle scar" stories at conventions and conferences.

These articles also noted the intense negative feelings of anger and frustration by health care givers (countertransference), usually after they expend exceptionally large amounts of time and energy coping with the patient, walking on eggshells around the patient only to have the patient get angry at them, flee the facility and later sue or file complaints against the staff. All of these emotions are also common in health-care givers who deal with any of the chronically and severely mentally-impaired. The health care provider should seek supervision if they become aware they are having any intense feelings about their patients, regardless of the diagnosis.

Some authors suggested using female therapist to counter negative transference toward the patient's mother (Schoenfeld et al., 1987). Intentional use of a male therapist at other times may also help with negative transference feelings if negative feelings about a female are too intense. The therapist sex can be adjusted to suit each patient's general status within a general range (meaning not getting changed every session). However good, clear and repeated framing of the therapy process early (almost immediately) in the treatment sessions regarding the transference/countertransference processes discussed and repeatedly discussed when difficulties arrive can serve the same purpose as therapist-switching.

In a separate perspective, Kannai (2009) avoided ever telling his patient the actual diagnosis (MbP) to avoid untoward upset.

On prognosis, Davidson et al. (2008) stated "The patient's prognosis depends upon the category under which the underlying disorder falls; depression and anxiety, for example, generally respond well to medication and/or cognitive behavioral therapy, whereas borderline personality disorder, like all personality disorders, is presumed to be pervasive and more stable over time." This author believes the actual diagnosis is not a potent predictor of prognosis since different therapists give different diagnoses to the same data. Old-time studies beyond the search parameters of this article reported that people with the best prognosis had acute conditions (sudden onset) as opposed to chronic (gradual onset), had family participating in therapy and were getting treatment close to home.

On a different prognostic factor, Carney (1980) (in Schoenfeld et al., 1987) reported that "nonambulatory" people (those who did not travel extensively to perpetrate) who did MbP had a better prognosis than people who were "ambulatory" (traveled from town to town, facility to facility). The extent of travel intuitively seems related to the desperation the perpetrator has to reoffend and/or avoid detection. Schoenfeld et al. (1987) also reported people who did voluntary participation in mental health programs showed better prognosis than those who did not participate at all or did so under greater duress.

Even one person with a combination of severe and chronic self-injury (self-induced burns, bacterial and fungus sepsis, interstitial cystitis, lead poisoning, esophageal and gastric ulcers, self-induced frostbite, fabricated sexual abuse, burning herself with oven cleaner, injecting herself with her feces, instilling clog remover into her bladder, boiling lead items and drinking the water, swallowing kitchen cleaner, and lacerating her vagina) was reportedly helped to be symptom/behavior free (Feldman, 2006) after about 16 months of therapy (but see immediately below).

Other Therapeutic Processes

There can be many therapeutic experiences in life, ranging from the most elaborate, planned therapeutic interventions to the spontaneous, unplanned insights and epiphanies. After many years of therapy, Feldman (2006) said his very difficult MS above-mentioned patient declared that the "central element" of her recovery was her getting religiously "born again" *after* her years-long therapy was finished. She said she was particularly moved by a passage in the Bible that said, "Do you not know that your body is a temple of the Holy Spirit, who is in you, whom you have received from God? You are not your own; you were bought at a price. Therefore, honor God with your body (1 Corinthians, 6: 19-20). One can speculate if her religious awakening would have occurred without the many years of secular care and comfort provide by physical and mental health care providers. This author is extremely pragmatic in analyzing therapeutic effectiveness in that he accepts good results from any source or method that relives suffering and affords objectively-measured higher quality of life for the victim and their families than pre-intervention.

Case Management Issues

Getting the suspected MS or MbP patient into therapy seems difficult enough. However, many separate case studies published indicated their behaviors after being hospitalized for psychological or psychiatric attention is difficult for the staff. Gregory and Jindal (2006) recommended the four following concerns be addressed in an in-depth handling of any suspected case of MS/MbP: 1) making the diagnosis, 2) use cognitive and behavioral framing, 3) team communication, and 4) avoidance of iatrogenic harm.

In regards to Item 2, this author believes cognitive-behavior therapy will only be effective and appropriate for the less severely impaired cases. Item three emphasizes the need for communication between all team members to minimize or circumvent any attempted manipulations by the patient. On the final factor (avoiding "iatrogenic harm") they wrote, "The clinician's attitude of giving the patient the benefit of the doubt provides no benefit to the patient and simply serves to help the clinician avoid difficult management issues. Psychiatric medications and procedures have obvious and potentially dangerous risks associated with them. In addition, prolonged and recurrent hospitalizations both maintain patients' dependency and dysfunction and reinforce a cycle of traumatic reenactment within the medical system of childhood abuse and abandonment issues. The physician is well advised to heed the dictum 'primum non nocere'". While that "do no harm" dictum has been the driving mentality for health care since the physical medical system was originated, the current mental health-care-giver needs to also have an "allow no harm" dictum for both forensic issues and malpractice issues. Both of these will be discussed in the sections below.

Many articles including Gregory and Jindal (2006) mention the issues of transference and countertransference in doing case management or therapy with the people having MS and MbP. The transference issue most frequently mentioned is the patient's reaction to being informed they have MS or MbP. They often react with denial, anger and shame to the point they frequently flee the facility, express negative feelings toward the health professional or file malpractice, ethics complaints or lawsuits against them. These are all typical reactions of chronically, severely mentally disordered people.

This transference can reach the level of a Borderline Personality Disorder "narcissistic rage" in terms of its irrational intensity. Mayo and Haggerty (1984) reported on a patient that became "silently enraged" when she saw her psychotherapist attending to another person while she was kept waiting. She soon checked herself into an inpatient psychiatric ward under pretense of being suicidally depressed because of a recent death of her boyfriend (note the symbolism of positive transference toward her therapist). Later she made another symbolic, factitious statement that her grandmother had died while mailing her a Christmas present. This also followed an incident where she viewed another therapist of hers being helpful to other patients. Note again the symbolism of the factitious story she concocted to her relationship with her therapist. As any therapist who has dealt with Borderline Personality people knows, the Borderlines are rarely silent in their rages. However, this borderline, hysterical emotional lability can be so intense as to trigger suicidal attempts in people accused of MbP to the point that some report 60% of all mothers accused of MbP attempt suicide (Artingstall, 1995).

Adler (1978) and Groves (1979) developed management protocols for the treatment and management of borderline patients in hospital settings. Regardless of the full and complete diagnoses of the MS/MbP person, their considerations are valuable to manage any difficult patient as many MS or MbP patients appear to be. Their steps included:

1) Early psychiatric consultation to help the staff understand the patient's behaviors and their role in his illness.
2) Re-establishment of open staff communication to prevent staff splitting (triangulation) and inconsistencies in the patient's day-to-day management.
3) Acknowledgement of the "real" stresses in the patient's situation and their relation to the patient's sense of entitlement.
4) Recognizing the primitive defense of the patient (splitting, identification, projection, identification, idealization, feelings of omnipotence and devaluation).
5) Empathic limit-setting without punishment or rejection.
6) Anticipation of repeated unrealistic expectations and regressive self-destructive acting-out after disappointment.

Feldman (2006) also recommended medical examinations on a regularly-scheduled basis to avoid appointments for contrived medical issues. This would reduce any emotional pressure the person had about their true physical health and minimize the effects that legitimate health concerns could have on pathological pressures for MS-related displacement.

Forensic Issues

Sometimes these cases reach the trial level, either civil or criminal. However, all professionals involved should document their efforts and observations in as objective and measurable terms as possible whether they believe they will be involved in litigation or not. Meadow, Schreier and Libow (1993) and Meadows (1985) have recommended a stepwise approach to the management of the legal (forensic) issues of this disorder summarized as follows:

1) Obtain and verify the victim's and the family's pertinent medical and social histories, previous hospitalizations, and medical records

2) Interview the other partner and any other family members alone, when the suspected perpetrator is not present
3) Admit the child to the hospital to observe the parent-child interaction, closely observe the suspected perpetrator, and determine the temporal relation between the symptoms and the perpetrator's presence
4) Consider separating the child from the suspected perpetrator to protect the child and to confirm cessation of the child's symptoms in the perpetrator's absence
5) During hospitalization and under close observation, obtain the necessary body-fluid samples for toxicology screens and any other relevant investigations; if a multidisciplinary team agrees on the procedure, hidden cameras can be used to record the interactions of the child and the suspected perpetrator in the hospital setting
6) Arrange for social service, psychological, and psychiatric evaluations of the child and the suspected perpetrator
7) Assemble a team or task force to examine the records objectively before the suspected perpetrator is confronted
8) Inform the local child protection and law enforcement agencies before confronting the suspected perpetrator
9) After the suspected perpetrator has been informed of the diagnosis, remove the child and other siblings at risk; for adequate protection, relocate the child to a place that is inaccessible to the suspected perpetrator
10) Recommend short-term and long-term psychological and psychiatric treatment for the suspected perpetrator[43]
11) Verify that long-term close monitoring will be provided by the court; this is essential for ensuring the child's safety
12) Ensure that relevant reunification criteria are met before the court considers reunification

Hospitalization of the perpetrator or the victim may be necessary to ensure that the two parties are both safe but are separated from each other. The clinician must attempt to understand the patient's disorder without becoming judgmental toward him or her; such negative judgments can hamper therapy. Indications for inpatient treatment include suicidal or homicidal ideations and grave disability (i.e., patients who are dangerous to themselves or others or who cannot care for themselves).

Activity should be restricted if patients pose a danger to themselves or others or if they are gravely disabled.

If patients are charged with a crime or if they have been arrested, they may be incarcerated.

Forensic psychological assessment has become a specialty in recent times with its utilization in the entire spectrum of criminal and civil litigation. There are books written on the subject (see Archer, 2006; Gacono and Evans, 2008; Jackson, 2008). However, this author wishes to emphasize the following errors that many mental health personnel commit in involvement with forensic issues:

1) Beware of the "imperfect fit" between the criminal judicial and the mental health professions. Most of the DSMs have this warning in the introduction section of them (see DSM-IV-TR, page xxxiii). The DSMs continue to state, "In most situations, the clinical diagnosis of the DSM mental disorder is not sufficient to establish the existence for legal purposes of a "mental disorder," "mental disability," "mental disease, "or "mental defect." In determining whether an individual meets a specified legal standard (e.g., for competence, criminal responsibility, or disability), additional information is usually required beyond that contained in the DSM diagnosis." That "additional information" varies state-to-state and is published in each state's laws on competence, criminal responsibility and disability.
The punch line: just because you give them a diagnosis from the DSM does not mean the judge is going to rule them "sane", "insane", "competent", "incompetent" or any variant thereof. The evidence has to meet the legal standard of that state for the judge to make the ruling. If not, your information may not be admitted.

2) "The diagnosis does not carry any necessary implications regarding the causes of the individual's mental disorder or its associated impairments...and does not require that there be knowledge about its etiology". (DSMs, Introduction). While this is in all DSMs I have direct access to (DSMIII through DSM-5), there are written but diluted assumptions about the cause of different diagnostic disorders. For example, much psychiatric information to the general public suggests that ADHD, Bipolar, Depression and Schizophrenia are genetically inherited. When any mental health authority provides information about diagnosis, there can be an overt or subliminal communication about your assumption of etiology. Be ready to defend your assumption of etiology because it can have massive impact on the final ruling by the court, especially as "mitigating circumstances". This consideration of mitigation comes into play after the guilty/not guilty (sentencing) phase. Any information can serve to "aggravate" (increase) or "mitigate" (ease) the harshness of the sentence. It can determine whether sentences run consecutively (stretched) or concurrently (stacked). It can determine if sentences can be suspended and diverted or served out.

3) Report only what you directly observe or have data on. Any other information you obtain from secondary informants is hearsay evidence and will probably not be admissible.

Other Caveats:

1) The Fatty Oxidation Disorder organization (fodsupport.org) posted an article titled "Munchausen by Proxy Perpetrator Profile or Warning Signs (quite different from diagnostic signs)". These comments are extremely critical but provide an insightful analysis of the warning signs for MbP and should be carefully considered during any

suspected case of MbP and *are in italics* after the classic warning signs of MbP. This author's will withhold all of his comments until the last response and those comments <u>will be underlined</u>.

- Primary caregiver, most often mother (99% of those accused are female). *This described 50% of the population and most caregivers. You can't profile on such a common characteristic. Fathers are often very involved in caregiving, if you ask.*

- Educated, middle to upper class. *Why should this be a bad thing? So why are more accusations against poor mothers? This group is more likely to appropriately consider doctors to be their hired consultants.*

- A highly attentive parent who is reluctant to leave her child's side and who herself seems to require constant attention. *This is entirely typical and appropriate for the parent of a sick child. Often they have to play the squeaky wheel. Children should NEVER be left alone in a hospital. Hospital personnel EXPECT parents to stay overnight and help care for the child. An overwhelmed and confused parent needs and deserves reassurance.*

- Friendly with medical staff and highly supportive and encouraging of staff. *Totally appropriate in this decade. Interestingly, many MSBP accusations are filed the day after the patient sues for malpractice.*

- Some medical background, most often nursing. *Most parents of sick children end up with an amazing level of medical knowledge. Nurses are more likely to be vocal advocates because they realize medicine is an inexact science.*

- Takes child to multiple physicians, moves frequently or transfers to another facility. *Seeking experts is completely normal and appropriate for the parent of a child with a difficult or undiagnosed condition. Many disease groups have documented an average of 6-10 physicians missing the diagnosis. Not all those missed diseases are rare ! (celiac) Families move due to job changes more frequently than in the past. Insurance changes can necessitate a change in physicians.*

- Refuses to accept changes in diagnosis or lack of diagnosis. *If an adult was in pain or feels terrible and told there is no reason for it, they would refuse to accept it. Why should parents accept the lack of a diagnosis?*

- Demands specific medical procedures or medications. *In this day and age, it is quite common and appropriate for patients to research test and treatments and request them. Pew Charitable Trust has research papers documenting this.*

- A parent who appears to be unusually calm in the face of serious difficulties. *Different parents have different coping styles and this should not be held against them. Project Delivery of Chronic Care sends medical residents to visit homebound, profoundly disabled children. The residents are usually completely astonished at how well and calmly many patients cope with situations that most people would consider intolerable.*

- A parent who is depressed or overwhelmed. *Again, a different coping style or a temporarily stage. Most parents of chronically ill get depressed at some point. Most are chronically overwhelmed. Getting help for depression is a positive step and should*

NEVER be used against the parent. Often a parent will realize they are depressed and overwhelmed but unable to take the time away from the child to care for their own health. Many fantasize about walking away. Remember the phrase, "It only takes a single child to raze a village."

- A parent who is angry and demanding. *Again, a different coping style/personality and sometimes appropriate or necessary to get the child help. Many parents get little sleep due to their child's illness. Women in particular may still be accused of being hysterical. In the old days, the favorite treatment for some childhood illnesses was Valium for the mother.*

- Marital problems, distant spouse. One spouse may spend extra time at work due to financial stress or may have to stay home with siblings. Marital stress is common even *with colic. With a chronic or mystery disease, if doctors disagree on treatments, so will the parents. Many fathers leave due to the chronic illness or death of a child. This should not be held against the remaining spouse who needs additional support. Spouses may naturally and subconsciously fall into the roles that don't fit your paradigm, yet they may be perfectly functional in a dysfunctional situation. Parents may take turns falling apart or keeping it together-an unwritten rule prevents them from coming unglued at the same time.*

- A parent dramatizes small crises or seems to have new crises continually. *As a way of getting your attention? Because life with a sick child IS full of crises? To laugh instead of crying? Is their Pissing and Moaning Quotient really that high or do they have many legitimate things to complain about? Parents of sick children get sick themselves easier, lose their keys and have minor traffic accidents more because they operate on overload every minute of every day. Complaining or talking about their stress is a good thing but we no longer encourage parents to do it with their child's doctor.*

- Welcomes tests, even if painful. *Knowing is almost always preferable to not knowing, even with cancer or fatal diseases.*

- Leaves out portions of medical history. *Long complicated histories need to be summarized. Dead ends or leads the parents don't put stock in may get left out.*

- Child's symptoms don't fit known diseases. *Medicine is full of mysteries and many people with rare diseases see dozens of doctors who don't recognize the pattern.*

- A child who has one or more medical problems that do not respond to treatment or that follow an unusual course that is persistent, puzzling and unexplained. *INDEPENDENT medical experts who have a flair for medical mysteries should review the ENTIRE medical record AND see the child with their own eye AND be allowed to talk freely to mom about the medical history and her theories.*

- Physical or laboratory findings that are highly unusual, discrepant with history, or physically or clinically impossible. *Children with metabolic diseases have 'impossible' lab results. Lab work should be carefully repeated and any odd results thoroughly researched before any action is taken. Video cameras should be used with EEG and apnea monitors. Toxicology results can be due to a chemically similar substance (epicac((sic)) and Benadryl) look the same on chromatography). A toxicology expert should be consulted.*

- Child has multiple hospitalizations. *Common in chronic illness.*
- Child's symptoms improve when away from mother. *Some diseases get better on their own or have a course that waxes and wanes unpredictably. A change in diet may fortuitously improve the symptoms in an allergy or metabolic situation. The change of symptoms is valid only if mother has trained the observer to watch for subtle changes. Children with rare diseases have become much sicker and even died when away from the mother. The CINA attorney should see the child and talk to the temporary caregivers frequently. Temporary caregivers MUST have the full medical information from the parents.*
- A family history of similar parental or sibling illness, unexplained sibling illness/death. *Many illnesses are genetic. Relatives may live for decades with mild symptoms. Patient associations should be consulted for possible genetic connections that are not yet published. For deaths many years ago, parents should be asked if they have a theory about the cause of death. A retrospective look at unexplained deaths is needed. Parents should be allowed to provide witnesses.*

This author's comments: all of these comments are extremely relevant to professional health-care givers and those involved in investigating suspected MbP as relevant to the false-positive issue. However, the experienced professional should be able to differentiate the parent of a truly chronically-ill, nonMbP parent from the MbP parent. The key will be in the extremes the MbP parent goes to dictate and trigger treatment and the deceitful manipulativeness of the MbP parent compared to the nonMbP parent. For example, simple omission of another medical examination or hospitalization is understandable in a parent dealing with a chronic and severely ill child. However, the omission of *all* previous examinations and hospitalizations by that parent is clear manipulation and deceit.

The most common subtle error this author has seen in diagnosis and detection of MbP is failure of the medical profession to clearly rule out all possible medical causes. This is no small task given the voluminous science on proven and suspected genetic disorders that is growing each week. Physical/genetic causes of the child's physical problems must be ruled before MbP can be accurately diagnosed. However, this author has also worked cases where the suspected MbP parents firmly reported to me that the child's problems were found by doctors to be due to an illness called "petechia". This disorder, of course, is the hemorrhage of small capillaries in the face and neck associated with attempted suffocation of the child. The reader will note that failure to identify genetic or congenital problems is one of the main errors that led to Dr. Meadows' professional difficulties (see below).

2) Health-care professionals are at higher risk of censure, complaints against their license and disbarment when dealing with forensic cases than those who merely due consulting, program development or education. Kaplan (2008) reported on the professional demise of Roy Meadow, the English pediatrician who published the first cases of MbP. Kaplan reported that Meadow shot to fame for his theories, becoming "a star witness" and was sought after near and far. However, he appeared to over-diagnose MbP in several cases that were overturned after the alleged perpetrator (usually women) had been incarcerated and lost their families. His reputation plunged. He also made the statement that the likelihood of two children in the same family dying of cot death was "1 in a million" when true statisticians reported it was as frequent as about 1 in 210. He was struck off the medical record (Britain's physician licensure board) for "serious medical misconduct" and criticized by a member of the House of Lords for "inventing a 'theory' without science". Most difficult for Meadow, the deaths of three of Sally Clark's children were shown on appeal to possibly have been due to congenital medical conditions. She had spent three years in prison before being exonerated. Other women had spent up to six years in prison due to his erroneous testimony.

On the good side, it became clear from Meadow's errors that a) the expert must confine themselves to the facts, b) avoid judgments they are not qualified to make, c) must stay within his professional discipline and d) not allow self-righteousness to intrude into a situation in which the court, not they, make a judgment.

It is of interest that Meadow's first wife, Gillian Paterson, described him as "a misogynist without any friends". While her opinion certainly has some subjective bias to it, she went on to write something else of importance to all health care providers: He "could not understand that MSBP was a rare diagnosis and he saw it wherever he looked". Kaplan accurately paralleled this overextension in MSBP with the overextension of later popular topics involving repressed memory and Dissociative Identity Disorder. This author can attest to that overextension in both of these later areas and has direct knowledge of one national expert on DID that did therapy on a woman who alleged she had a murderous cannibalistic alter-personality who had killed and eaten over 100 victims in her rural community. As the therapy progressed and her husband and family got involved, they and the local sheriff started researching those alleged murders and found no murders in their community or surrounding areas, much less any that involved cannibalization. When this was discovered, the expert was successfully sued for malpractice, lost his license to practice and his credentialing. From this tragedy, one must remember that the expert must focus on and confine themselves to *substantiated* facts in their area of expertise.

State agencies such as social services, child protective services or division of family services get involved in many MS or MbP cases at various points. In August, 2002, the British Department of Health published definitive guidance on safeguarding children. This was called Safeguarding Children in Whom Illness is Fabricated or Induced (DoH 2002) and its publication followed a year-long public consultation exercise during which the health department invited comment on a document entitled Safeguarding Children in Whom Illness is Induced or Fabricated by Carers with Parenting Responsibilities (DoH 2001), which was supplementary to Working Together to Safeguard Children (DoH 1999). Some of these considerations are relevant no matter what country the child and alleged perpetrator live in and are similar to guidelines in the American states of Michigan and Indiana this author has reviewed.

In one part of the British Department of Health guidance it is written, "Such is (the parents') deviousness that it is dangerous for professionals to make their concerns explicit before they have sufficient evidence to ensure the adequate protection of the child." This perspective is consistent with most American mandated-reporter demands that only require the professional to have a reasonable degree of concern before they report suspected child abused of MbP or other means. Most if not all American states also provide some protection from frivolous lawsuits against any health care provider or social services agent from civil or criminal complaint if they have acted in good faith. This same guidance then stated "It is important for the agencies with statutory responsibilities to seek expert advice before they invite such family members to engage in decision making or any level of partnership." This attitude varies from the American cases this author has handled in that American states allow the family members, even those suspected of dire misbehaviors, to engage in decision making at all levels until or when their parental rights are terminated.

In another part it is written, "The guidance is not explicit concerning the level of evidence required in terms of protecting the child. This is a major flaw as clinicians will still be faced with dilemmas concerning what is a sufficient level of evidence to protect the child. For example, will the expert opinion of paediatricians, backed by a careful analysis of the child medical record, be sufficient?" This author does not believe that is a great concern for mental health providers since the judge will make the final ruling as to the admissibility and relevance of any and all evidence. The health care worker is mostly obligated to share the plain facts as they know it and not present hearsay evidence as fact. It is also a minor issue since currently the opinions of all physical and mental health professionals in America are weighed before the judge makes their decision.

Bibliography

Adler, G. (1973). Hospital treatment of borderline patients. *American Journal of Psychiatry*, 130, 32-36.

Altman, J.S. & Gardner, G.M. (1998). Cervicofacial subcutaneous emphysema in a patient with Munchausen syndrome. *Ear, Nose, & Throat Journal*, 77 (6), pp. 476, 481-2.

Al-Owain M., Al-Zaidan, H., Al-Hashem, A., Kattan, H., & Al-Dowaish, A. (2009). Munchausen syndrome by proxy mimicking as Gaucher disease. *European Journal Of Pediatrics*, Vol. 169 (8), pp. 1029-32.

Archambault-Grenier, M.A., Roy, J., Beauchemin, N., Cohen, S., Lachance, S., & Kiss, T. (2010). Munchausen's syndrome in the allogeneic stem cell transplantation setting: a rare but potentially devastating condition. *Bone Marrow Transplantation*, 45 (3), pp. 600-1.

Artingstall, K.A. (1995). Munchausen Syndrome by Proxy. *FBI Law Enforcement Bulletin*, 64, 5-11.

Asher, R.A.J. (1951). Munchausen's Syndrome. *Lancet*, Feb 10;1(6650):339-41

Avigal, A. & Hall, T.G. (2012). *Secrets Unraveled: Overcoming Munchausen Syndrome. Publisher unknown.*

Azodo, B. & Esen, U. (2002). Munchausen's syndrome with predilection [correction of predeliction] for gynaecology.: The Journal Of *Journal Of Obstetrics And Gynaecology The Institute Of Obstetrics And Gynaecology*, 22(3), 331.

Bandura, A. (1977). Social Learning Theory. Englewood Cliffs, NJ: Prentice Hall.

Barker, J.C. (1962). The Syndrome of Hospital Addiction (Munchausen's Syndrome). *Journal of Mental Science*, 108, 167-182.

Bauer, M., & Boegner, F. (1996). Neurological syndromes in factitious disorder. *Journal of Nervous & Mental Disease*, 184, 281– 288.

Bappal, B., George, M., Nair, R., Khusaiby, S.A. & De Silva, V. (2001) Factitious hypoglycemia: a tale from the Arab world. *Pediatrics*, 107 (1), pp. 180-1.

Bass, E. & Davis, L. (1994). *The Courage to Heal* (3rd ed.), Harper & Row; NYNY.

Beckford-Ball, J. (2000). Patients deserve trust not surveillance cameras. *British Journal Of Nursing.*9 (10), pp. 608.

Beis, J.M., Bertoni, N., Isner-Horobeti, M.E., Kandel. M., Mainard, D., Martinet, N., Chapelain, L.L., & Paysant, J. Factitious torsion dystonia in rehabilitation: a singular new case and literature review. *NeuroRehabilitation*, Vol. 30 (3), pp. 235-7.

Berberoğlu M; Ocal G; Cetinkaya E; Ikincioğullari A; Babacan E; Kansu A; Adiyaman P; Akçurin S; Memioğlu N. (2000). Polyglandular autoimmune syndrome accompanied by Munchausen syndrome. *Pediatrics International: Official Journal Of The Japan Pediatric Society,.* 42 (4), pp. 386-8;

http://www.whonamedit.com/doctor.cfm/1082.html. Accessed 6 June 2014.

Bensler, J.M. & Paauw, D.S., Apotemnophilia masquerading as medical morbidity. *Southern Medical Journal*, 96 (7), pp. 674-6.

Bools, C., Neale, B., & Meadow, R. (1994). Munchausen syndrome by proxy: A study of psychopathology. *Child Abuse and Neglect*, 18, 769– 771.

Bulik, C.M., Sullivan, P.F., Fear, J.L. & Pickering, A. (1996). A case of comorbid anorexia nervosa, bulimia nervosa, and Munchausen's syndrome. *The International Journal Of Eating Disorders*, 20 (2), pp. 215-8.

Bursten, B. (1965). On Munchausen's Syndrome. Archives of General Psychiatry, 13:261.

Carney, M.W.P. (1980). Artefactual Illness to Attract Medical Attention. *British Journal of Psychiatry*, 136: 542-47.

Caocci, G., Pisu, S. & La Nasa, G, A simulated case of chronic myeloid leukemia: the growing risk of Munchausen's syndrome by internet. *Leukemia & Lymphoma*, 49 (9), pp. 1826-8.

Chiczewski, D. & Kelly, M. (2003). Munchausen Syndrome by Proxy: The Importance of Behavioral Artifacts. FBI Law Enforcement Bulletin 72 (7), 21-24.

Concepcion, S.B. & Garcia-Alba, C. (2008). Munchausen Syndrome: A dilemma for diagnosis. *Rorschachiana*, 29(2), 183-200.

Cramer, B.C., Gershberg, R.M and Stern, M. (1971). Munchausen patient-physician relationship. *Archives of General Psychiatry*, 24, 573-578.

Davidson, G. et al. (2008). Abnormal Psychology - 3rd Canadian Edition. Mississauga: John Wiley & Sons Canada, Ltd. p. 412.

Denny, S.J., Grant, C.C., Pinnock, R. (2001). Epidemiology of Munchausen syndrome by proxy in New Zealand. *Journal Of Paediatrics And Child Health*, 37 (3), pp. 240-3.

Diagnostic and Statistical Manual-5 Desk Reference (2013). American Psychiatric Association, Washington, D.C.

Dute, J. (2003). European Court of Human Rights. ECHR 2003/4 case of Venema v. The Netherlands, 17 December 2002, no. 3573/97 (second section). *European Journal Of Health Law*, 10 (3), pp. 320-3

EisendrathS. J., & McNiel, D. E. (2002). Factitious disorders in civil litigation: Twenty cases illustrating the spectrum of abnormal illness-affirming behavior. *Journal of the American Academy of Psychiatry & the Law*, 30, 391– 399.

Feldman, K.W., Feldman, M.D., Grady, R., Burns, M.W. & McDonald, R. (2007). Renal and urologic manifestations of pediatric condition falsification/Munchausen by proxy. *Pediatric Nephrology*, 22 (6), pp. 849-56.

Feldman, M. (2006). Recovery from Munchausen Syndrome. Southern Medical Association, 99(12).

Fisher, Jill A (2006). Investigating the Barons: narrative and nomenclature in Munchausen syndrome. *Perspectives in Biology and Medicine,* 49 (2): 250–62. Retrieved 6 June 2014.

Fujiwara, T., Okuyama, M., Kasahara, M., & Nakamura, A. Differences of Munchausen syndrome by proxy according to predominant symptoms in Japan. *Pediatrics International: Official Journal Of The Japan Pediatric Society,* 50 (4), pp. 537-40.

Gilligan, C. (1981). In a different voice. Cambridge, MA. Harvard University Press.

Gross, B. (2008). Caretaker Cruelty: Munchausen's and Beyond. From http://www.theforensicexaminer.com/archive/summer08/4/. Accessed June 6 2014.

Groves, G.E. (1975). Management of the borderline patient on a medical or surgical ward: the psychiatric consultant's role. International Journal of Psychiatric Medicine, 6, 333-348.

Guler N Tochigi, M., Hara, H., Goshima. J., Kobayashi. M., Shimizu, H., Yokoyama,A., Matsunaga, A., Takemura, T., & Terui, T. (2007). Cutaneous Munchausen's syndrome caused by self-injections of fermented beans. Journal Of The European Academy Of Dermatology And Venereology, 22 (7), pp. 886-7.

Gregory, R.J. &Jindal, S. (2006). Factitious disorder on an inpatient psychiatry ward. *The American Journal Of Orthopsychiatry,* 76(1). Accessed June 6 2014.

Hall, D.E., Eubanks, L., Meyyazhagan, L.S., Kenney, R.D. & Johnson, S.C. (2000). Evaluation of covert video surveillance in the diagnosis of munchausen (sic) syndrome by proxy: lessons from 41 cases. 105 (6), pp. 1305-12. Accessed 13 June 2014.

Highland, K.B. & Flume, P.A. (2002). A "story" of a woman with cystic fibrosis. *Chest,* 121 (5), pp. 1704-7.

Honjo, S. (1996). A mother's complaints of overeating by her 25-month-old daughter: a proposal of anorexia nervosa by proxy. *The International Journal Of Eating Disorders,* 20 (4), pp. 433-37.

Hood, B.M. & Harbord, M.G., Paediatric narcolepsy: complexities of diagnosis. *Journal Of Paediatrics And Child Health,.* 38 (6), pp. 618-21.

Kannai, R. (2009). Munchausen by mommy. *Systems & Health: The Journal Of Collaborative Family Healthcare,* 27 (1).

Kaplan, R. (2008). Savonarola at the stake: the rise and fall of Roy Meadow. *Bulletin Of Royal Australian And New Zealand College Of Psychiatrists,* 16 (3), pp. 213-5.

Krause, K.E (1886), "Münchhausen, Hieronimus Karl Friedrich Freiherr von", Allgemeine Deutsche Biographie (ADB) (in German) 23, Leipzig: Duncker & Humblot, pp. 1–5.

Kareem, S.T. (2012). "Fictions, Lies, and Baron Munchausen's Narrative". *Modern Philology* 109 (4): 483–509. doi:10.1086/665538. Retrieved 9 June 2014.

Klepper, J., Heringhaus, A., Wurthmann, C., & Voit, T. (2008). Expect the unexpected: favourable outcome in Munchausen by proxy syndrome. *European Journal Of Pediatrics* 167 (9), pp. 1085-8.

Kume, K. & Sakata, H. (2010). Education and imaging. Gastrointestinal: colonic foreign bodies needing surgical removal. *Journal Of Gastroenterology And Hepatology*, 25 (4), pp. 839.

Kokturk, N., Ekim, N., Aslan, S., Kanbay, A., Acar, A.T. (2006). A rare cause of hemoptysis: factitious disorder. *Southern Medical Journal*, Vol. 99 (2), pp. 186-7.

Lee, J.C., Lin, K.L., Lin, J.J., Hsia, S.H., Wu, C.T. (2010). Non-accidental chlorpyrifos poisoning-an unusual cause of profound unconsciousness. *European Journal Of Pediatrics,*169 (4), pp. 509-11.

Leeder, E. (1990). Supermom or child abuser? Treatment of the Munchausen mother. *Women and Therapy*, 9(4), 69-98.

Leiba, A., Capua, M., Dinour, D., Adir, E., Sela, B., & Holzman, E. (2012). Nephrotic range proteneuria and hypertension-which came first? *Kidney International,* 82, 612.

Masterson, J., Dunsworth, R. & Williams, N. (1988). Extreme illness exaggeration in pediatric patients: A variant of Munchausen's by proxy? American Journal of Orthopsychiatry, 58, 188-195.

Meadow, R. (1977). Munchausen syndrome by proxy: The hinterland of child abuse. *Lancet*, 2(8033), 343-345.

Meadow R. (1985). Management of Munchausen syndrome by proxy. Archives of Disabled Children, 60(4):385-93.

Meadow, R. (1987). Munchausen syndrome by proxy abuse perpetrated by men. *Archives of Disabled Children*. 78, 210-16. Retrieved from http://adc.bmj.com/content/78/3/210.full on 19 June 2014.

Millon Adolescent Clinical Inventory. (1996). Pearson Education, Inc. Minneapolis, MN.

Millon Clinical Multiaxial Inventory III. (1994). Pearson Education, Inc. Minneapolis, MN.

Minnesota Multiphasic Personality Inventory®-2 (MMPI®-2), University of Minnesota, 1989.

Munchausen by Proxy Perpetrator Profile or Warning Signs (quite different from diagnostic signs) at fodsupport.org. Retrieved 8 June 2014.

"Munchausen Overview" at fhttp://health.howstuffworks.com/mental-health/mental-disorders/munchausen2.htm. Retrieved 6 June 2014.

"Munchausen Syndrome" at http://www.medicinenet.com/munchausen_syndrome/article.htm. Retrieved 7 of May 2014.

Okuniewska, A., Walczuk, B.I., Czubek, M., & Biernat, W. (2011). Recurrent deep ulcers resembling rare cancers as a form of factitious disorder. *Acta Dermato-Venereologica,* Vol. 91 (3), pp. 341-2.

Park, T.A., Borsch, M.A., Dyer, A.R. & Peiris, A.N. (2004). Cardiopathia fantastica: the cardiac variant of Munchausen syndrome. *Southern Medical Journal,* 97 (1), pp. 48-52

Patterson, R., Schatz, M. & Horton, M. (1974). Munchausen's stridor: non-organic laryngeal obstruction. Clinical Allergy, 4 (3), pp. 307-10.

Raspe, E.R. (2007). The Surprising Adventures of Baron Munchausen. Wilder Publications, Redford VA.

Safeguarding children from fabricated or induced illness. (2002). *Nursing Management,* 1354-5760, 9(7).

Schoenfeld, H., Margolin, J. & Baum, S. (1987). Munchausen Syndrome As A Suicide Equivalent: Abolition of the Syndrome by Psychotherapy. *American Journal of Psychotherapy,* 41(4).

Schreier, H.A., Libow, J.A., eds. (1993). *Hurting for Love: Munchausen by Proxy Syndrome.* New York, NY: Guilford; 1993.

Swanson, D.A. (1981). The Munchausen Syndrome. American Journal of Psychotherapy, 35(3), 436-446.

Tamay, Z., Akcay, A., Kilic, G., Peykerli, G., Devecioglu, E. & Ones, U. (2007). Corrosive poisoning mimicking cicatricial pemphigoid: Munchausen by proxy. *Child: Care, Health And Development,* 33 (4), pp. 496-9.

Tasic, V., Korneti, B., Cakalaroski, K. & Korneti, P. (2005). Factitious proteinuria fabricated with adding human albumin: how to detect it? *Pediatric Nephrology,* 20 (6), pp. 840-1

The Munchausen by Proxy Perpetrator Profile or Warning Signs (quite different from diagnostic signs) at http://fodsupport.org/pdf/Parent_Comments_to_MSBP_Perpetrator_Profile.pdf. Accessed 21 June 2014.

Tran, H.A. (2006). A woman with malaise and hyponatremia. Hyponatremia factitia (Munchausen syndrome) secondary to desmopressin use. *Archives Of Pathology & Laboratory Medicine,* 130 (2), pp. e15-8.

Tüfekçi Ö; Yilmaz, S., Karapinar, T.H., Gozmen, S., Cakmakci, H., Hiz, S., Irken, G., & Oren, H. (2011). *Pediatric Hematology And Oncology* Vol. 28 (6), pp. 517-22;

Warner, J.O. (2005). Child protection and allergy. *Pediatric Allergy And Immunology: Official Publication Of The European Society Of Pediatric Allergy And Immunology,* 16 (8), pp. 621

Wenk, R.E. (2003). Molecular evidence of Munchausen syndrome by proxy. *Archives Of Pathology & Laboratory Medicine,* 127 (1), pp. e36-7.

Yuan, C., Liu, H., Fu, X., Yu, X., Yu, G., Fao, F., Lu, N., Li, J.,Liu, J., Tian, H., & Zhang, F. (2012). Munchausen by proxy in a family. Indian Journal of Dermatology, Verenology and Leprosy. November-December, 78(6), 748-752.

Vaught, W. & Fleetwood, J. (2002). Covert video surveillance in pediatric care. The Hastings Center Report 32 (6), pp. 10-1. Accessed 13 June 2014.

Zibis, A.H., Dailiana, Z.H., Papaliaga, M.N., Vrangalas, V.A., Mouzas, O.D., & Malizos, K.N. (2010). Munchausen syndrome: A differential diagnostic trap for hand surgeons. *Journal Of Plastic Surgery And Hand Surgery,* Vol. 44 (4-5), pp. 222-4.

www.ingramcontent.com/pod-product-compliance
Lightning Source LLC
Chambersburg PA
CBHW070238290526
45789CB00004B/1679